STARTING SPORT

Karate

Rebecca Hunter

Photography by Chris Faircloug

D0229118

W
FRANKLIN WATTS

ALIS
2664139

First published in 2009 by
Franklin Watts
338 Euston Road
London NW1 3BH

Franklin Watts Australia
Level 17/207 Kent Street
Sydney NSW 2000

© 2009 Franklin Watts

ISBN: 978 0 7496 8945 2

ABERDEENSHIRE LIBRARY AND	
INFORMATION SERVICES	
2664139	
HJ	2506108
J796.815	£11.99
JU	JNF

Dewey classification number: 796.815'3

All rights reserved. No part of this publication may be reproduced, stored in a retrieval system, or transmitted in any form or by any means, electronic, mechanical, photocopying, recording or otherwise, without the prior written permission of the copyright owner.

A CIP catalogue record for this book is available from the British Library.

Planning and production by Discovery Books Limited
Editor: Rebecca Hunter
Designer: Ian Winton
Photography: Chris Fairclough
Additional photography: Istockphoto.com: p.21 (Gerville Hall); Shutterstock: p.12 (GeoM); p.22 bottom (Lucian Coman); cover and title page frieze, 2nd and 5th image (Lucian Coman).

Consultant: Chris Mileham, 6th Dan

The author, packager and publisher would like to thank the following people for their participation in this book: Barbi Mileham and the students of the Shitoryu Shukokai Union Shrewsbury Club.

Printed in China

Franklin Watts is a division of Hachette Children's Books, an Hachette UK company.

www.hachette.co.uk

Contents

Introduction to karate

The martial art of karate started on the Japanese island of Okinawa hundreds of years ago. The word *karate* means 'empty hand'. It is a form of fighting that uses no weapons.

People who practise karate are called *karateka*. They use a combination of blocks, strikes, locks and throws to beat their opponent.

Karate kit

Karate is practised wearing an outfit called a *gi*. This consists of a thin, white cotton jacket and trousers. A belt is tied around the waist. Girls should wear a white T-shirt under their jacket.

It is important to keep your gi clean and well-ironed. Karateka should always look smart and neatly dressed.

Karate grades

Each karateka wears a coloured belt to denote their grade. You will start with a white belt and progress through 8 grades or *kyu* before you get to your first black belt. The belt order is yellow (8th kyu), orange (7th kyu), green (6th kyu), blue (5th kyu), purple (4th kyu) and brown (3rd, 2nd and 1st kyu) then black. There are also stages within the black belt called *dans*, so a new black belt is a 1st dan, and the most experienced is a 10th dan.

The dojo

Dojo is the name given to the place where karateka learn 'the way' of karate. A karate teacher is called a **sensei**.

Personal development

Because karate training is about combat, you must learn the importance of respect and self-control. Before a training session, you need to prepare mentally. You will spend about one minute meditating with your eyes closed.

Like in all martial arts, karateka show each other great respect. It is customary to bow to your sensei and each other before and after training together and also when entering or leaving the dojo.

Protection

For some *kumite* sessions (see page 24), you will need to wear equipment to protect yourself. This consists of mitts for the hands, and shin and instep protectors for the legs and feet. In a competition, a pair of opponents will wear red and blue belts and matching protectors.
Gum shields should also be worn.

Safety in the dojo

Karateka must behave responsibly at all times so you do not injure yourself or anyone else.
• All jewellery including earrings and watches must be removed.
• Long hair must be tied back.
• Fingernails and toenails must be kept short.
• ALWAYS do as your sensei asks immediately.

Kihon 1 Stances and blocks

Kihon is a Japanese word meaning 'basics'. In karate it refers to the many basic techniques that karateka must master. Kihon may be practised alone or in groups or pairs.

Stances

Karateka learn many stances. These give you good balance and control. This helps you to avoid being hit and to attack back quickly.

The horse-riding stance (right) or ***kiba-dachi***, enables you to lower your centre of gravity while maintaining a good posture.

The cat stance (left), or ***nekoashi-dachi***, provides the agility needed in combat.

Blocks

To defend against an attack, you need to learn how to deflect or block the opponent.

The forearm block (right) is a simple inward block normally used to protect the middle body area. It is made by pulling your inner forearm across the front of your body from the outside towards the inside.

The rising block (below) is used to defend the head from various attacks. It can be used for defending against an attack with a weapon. To do the rising block move the bent, blocking arm diagonally across your chest. Then raise it straight up above your head. The outer forearm is used to do the block and you must make sure that it is above your head height.

Kihon 2 Punches

A punch is a strike made using the fist.

Making a fist

The fist must be made very tightly and the thumb should not be enclosed by the fingers. If this is not done correctly, you are likely to injure your own hand rather than your opponent!

Punches must be fast and strong and on target. Impact is usually made with the knuckles of the index and middle finger.

When you are practising punches you should stop short of actually touching your training partner, so they are not hurt.

There are many punching techniques. Two examples are the basic reverse punch and the backfist.

Reverse punch

The reverse punch, or *gyaku-tsuki*, is one of the most effective of all punches. It can be done with great power, speed and accuracy.

Here the karateka steps forward onto his left foot and punches with his right fist. The power

of the punch comes from the fist, wrist, elbow and hip all working together. The karateka above is aiming for a part of his opponent's body called the solar plexus. You should always practise punching with both hands.

Backfist

The backfist, or *uraken*, is used when fighting close to your opponent. It is used to punch vulnerable areas such as the bridge of the nose. The blow comes not from below but in a circular action from the elbow. The fist is snapped forward from the wrist to increase impact.

kihon 3 – kicks

A kick is a strike made using the foot. Kicks are useful because they allow you to stay further away from your opponent. Impact is made with a different part of the foot depending on the type of kick used: the ball, the instep, the heel or the side – but never with the toes as these are easily injured.

Karateka learn to kick to the front, back and side. Some kicks made are in a straight line, others may be circular or involve spins or jumps. There are many kicking techniques but the basic ones are the front kick, side kick, back kick and roundhouse kick.

Front kick
The kick you are most likely to learn first is the front kick or **mae-geri**.

1. Begin in the starting position known as **kamae**.

2. Lift your knee and prepare your foot by pulling your toes back.

The roundhouse kick

One of the most popular kicks is the roundhouse or **mawashi-geri**. This is a circular kick that can be used to strike into the side of your opponent.

1. Begin in the starting position, kamae. Raise your knee and point your toes, while pivoting on your other foot.

2. Snap your raised leg forward in an arc towards your opponent's head and aim to strike with the top of your foot (instep). Keep your elbows close to your sides.

3. Thrust your lower leg forward towards your target. Aim to kick them with the ball of your foot. Keep your hands up to guard your face.

4. Return your leg quickly to the starting position, to prevent being caught off balance.

Other techniques

Many parts of the body can be used in self-defence. Everyone has heard of the 'karate chop'! Really this is an open handed strike called **shuto-uchi**. It can be used in many ways, for example as a defence move against a person with a weapon.

As your opponent goes to strike you, move to the side and then strike their wrist with the fleshy part of the side of your hand.

You are aiming to hit the tendons in their wrist. This will be extremely painful and they will drop their weapon.

Elbow strike

The elbow strike is called *empi-uchi* and is one of the strongest strikes that can be delivered in a variety of different ways with great power. There is little danger of injury because elbows are strong bones. This means they can be useful weapons especially for close-up strikes.

Avoiding your opponent, move in while raising your arm across your chest. The strike is sideways with the point of the elbow aiming for the opponent's sternum, or breastbone.

Sweeps and throws

Most karate moves involve strikes to the upper body. However, sweeps and throws are used to unbalance the opponent by sweeping their legs from under them and throwing them to the floor.

Foot sweep

The foot sweep, or **ashi-barai**, is an effective way of surprising your opponent.

Using the bottom of your foot, perform a strong, low sweeping or scooping action to one of your opponent's legs. This should cause the opponent to lose balance and fall to the floor. When they have fallen, you should follow the move quickly with a counterstrike such as a reverse punch.

Hip throw

Often in a combat situation you can end up fighting close to your opponent. It is important to be able to throw them to the floor. One such throw is the hip throw, or *ogoshi*.

When grappling with an opponent, the karateka swiftly steps diagonally across in front of his opponent, turning his back to the opponent and wrapping his arm around the opponent's waist. Continuing the turning movement, the karateka straightens his legs and pulls his opponent over his hips. He should control the landing onto the floor.

Power

In karate training you constantly work to improve the power of your striking techniques. The aim is to achieve maximum power at the exact moment of impact. This focusing of power is known as **kime**.

Padwork

One way of improving power is to train using pads. You punch, kick and strike pads to build up your speed, strength, stamina and improve kime. A partner will take it in turns to hold the pads for you.

Here a karateka practises an elbow strike using a pad.

A roundhouse kick can be dangerous. It is best to practise it with a pad.

Kiai

You need a strong spirit and a positive mental attitude in karate. One way to build spirit and focus power is to *kiai*. This is the shout that you cry when making a strike. It sounds like 'Ee-ya!' and helps you to maximise the release of energy into the strike at the right time. Using a strong kiai when you attack will build your courage while helping to scare your opponent.

Kata

Kata means 'pattern', or 'form', and is a very important part of karate training. A kata is a series of movements done in a set pattern.

You will learn all the moves of the kata by repeating them many times. They are done without a partner – it is like training with an imaginary opponent.

Performing on your own allows you to pay attention to every detail of each move such as stance, posture and the hand and foot positions.

All kata moves represent self-defence. These pictures show karateka performing moves from different katas. In both pictures the outstretched arm represents a shuto-uchi strike to the neck. The other hand is deflecting a punch – to the head (above) or the body (left).

It is fun and helpful to practise the kata moves together as a group. The sensei will help correct any small mistakes that you might make.

Bunkai

It is important to learn what all the moves of a kata represent and then practise them with a real opponent. After learning their katas, karateka will train with a partner and practise deflecting a punch and counter-attacking with a shuto-uchi strike. Understanding and practising kata moves with a partner is known as **bunkai**.

Kumite

Kumite means fighting. The kumite section of karate involves sparring with a partner.

One-step fighting

One-step fighting, or *ippon kumite*, is an exercise used to prepare the karateka for kumite practice. A karateka will attack another with just one punch or kick that is chosen by the sensei. The defender will block the attack and perform a counterattack.

Here, a karateka performs a roundhouse kick. The other karateka has managed to block and catch the kick and is performing a reverse punch to the opponent's stomach as a counterattack.

Free fighting

After you have mastered one-step fighting you will be able to move on to free fighting, or *jiyu kumite*. Here, both karateka are free to perform any attacking technique or combination of techniques at any moment. Both karateka must be ready to defend and counterattack at any time.

Body protection

Free fighting is performed at all times with total control to avoid injury, and protection must be worn by all students.

This karateka is performing a controlled front kick to his opponent's body.

Competitions

There are both kata and kumite competitions. Both are divided into different categories to ensure safety and fairness for all ages, sizes, grades and ability.

Kata competitions

In kata competitions, karateka may compete either as individuals or in teams of three. They must perform a nominated kata in front of judges. The judges will look for good form and posture, correct speed, power, focus and grace, to decide which competitor is best.

In a team event, the karateka must attempt to perform all the moves at the same time as each other, as well as making sure all the moves are done in exactly the right way.

Kumite competitions

These are free-fighting competitions and, for safety reasons, competitors are divided into categories depending on their grade and height and weight.

Here two karateka are in a kumite match. One (in red) is performing a reverse punch to the other's stomach. The seated judge is indicating that he thinks it is a good scoring punch by showing his red flag. The referee is stopping the match so that he can award a point to the red competitor.

At the end of a competition the winner is presented with a medal or trophy to mark their achievement.

Karate terms

ashi-barai foot sweep

bunkai practising kata moves with a partner

dans stages within the black belt

dojo the hall where karate is practised

empi-uchi elbow strike

gi the outfit worn to do karate

gyaku-tsuki reverse punch

ippon kumite one-step fighting

jiyu kumite free fighting

kamae the starting position

karate empty hand

karateka a person who practises karate

kata a sequence of movements

kiai the shout made when making a strike

kiba-dachi horse-riding stance

kihon the basic moves

kime effective focusing of power

kumite fighting

kyu grades

mae-geri front kick

mawashi-geri roundhouse kick

nekoashi-dachi cat stance

ogoshi hip throw

sensei a karate teacher

shuto-uchi open handed strike

uraken backfist

Further reading

How to Improve at Karate, Ashley P Martin, Crabtree Publishing Company, 2007

The Shotokan Karate Handbook: Beginner to Black Belt, Gursharan Sahota, Gursharan Sahota, 2005

Karate: Combat Sports, Clive Gifford, Franklin Watts, 2008

Karate: Get Going Martial Arts, Neil Morris, Heinemann Library, 2002

The Young Martial Arts Enthusiast, David Mitchell, Dorling Kindersley, 1997

Further information

English Karate Federation
23 Sidlaws Road, Cove
Farnborough, Hampshire
GU14 9JL
Email: info@englishkaratefederation.com
Website:
    www.englishkaratefederation.com

Shotokan Karate Association
22 Elmsdale Road
Wootton, Bedfordshire
MK43 9JN
Website: www.shotokankarate.org.uk

Australian Karate Federation Inc.
5 Stuart Street
Moonee Ponds VIC 3039
Website: www.akf.com.au/

Goshin Ryu Karate Australia
P.O. Box 547
Manly 2095
Email: goshinryu@goshinryu.com
Website: www.goshinryu.com

Index

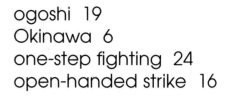